CW00521327

Daily Intentions

Intentions invite the Universe to show you which direction to take. They allow you to focus on who you are here and now and where you want to go.

Find time each morning to sit, breath and relax into your thoughts. Use this Daily Intention Journal to guide you down the path of things you want rather than the things you do not want without censoring your thoughts.

You may wish to use a different intention every day or you may wish to use the same one for a week or month at a time. The choice is yours!

At the end of every week, there are pages to record and reflect on your intentions to help guide you into a new week. These reflections are optional but do help to check in with yourself to make sure you are moving in the right direction.

DAILY INTENTION

Date: /   /

Questions to ask yourself today

- What do I need today?
- What is my why?
- What Inspires me?
- What is my heart's deepest desire?
- What do I need to do in order to succeed?
- What obstacles do I need to overcome if any and how will I do this?

> *Space for thoughts & feelings*

> **Intention of the Day**

Daily Reflection

- What have I done today to commit to my intention?

_____

- Today I am grateful for?

_____

_____

- Today_____brought me joy.

DAILY INTENTION

Date: /   /

Questions to ask yourself today

- What do I need today?
- What is my why?
- What Inspires me?
- What is my heart's deepest desire?
- What do I need to do in order to succeed?
- What obstacles do I need to overcome if any and how will I do this?

Space for thoughts & feelings

Intention of the Day

Daily Reflection

- What have I done today to commit to my intention?

_____

- Today I am grateful for?

_____

_____

- Today_____brought me joy.

DAILY INTENTION

Date: / /

Questions to ask yourself today

- What do I need today?
- What is my why?
- What Inspires me?
- What is my heart's deepest desire?
- What do I need to do in order to succeed?
- What obstacles do I need to overcome if any and how will I do this?

Space for thoughts & feelings

Intention of the Day

Daily Reflection

- What have I done today to commit to my intention?

_____

- Today I am grateful for?

_____

_____

- Today_____brought me joy.

DAILY INTENTION

Date: /   /

Questions to ask yourself today

- What do I need today?
- What is my why?
- What Inspires me?
- What is my heart's deepest desire?
- What do I need to do in order to succeed?
- What obstacles do I need to overcome if any and how will I do this?

Space for thoughts & feelings

Intention of the Day

Daily Reflection

- What have I done today to commit to my intention?

_____

- Today I am grateful for?

_____

_____

- Today_____brought me joy.

DAILY INTENTION

Date: /   /

Questions to ask yourself today

- What do I need today?
- What is my why?
- What Inspires me?
- What is my heart's deepest desire?
- What do I need to do in order to succeed?
- What obstacles do I need to overcome if any and how will I do this?

Space for thoughts & feelings

Intention of the Day

Daily Reflection

- What have I done today to commit to my intention?

_____

- Today I am grateful for?

_____

_____

- Today_____brought me joy.

DAILY INTENTION

Date: /   /

Questions to ask yourself today

- What do I need today?
- What is my why?
- What Inspires me?
- What is my heart's deepest desire?
- What do I need to do in order to succeed?
- What obstacles do I need to overcome if any and how will I do this?

Space for thoughts & feelings

Intention of the Day

Daily Reflection

- What have I done today to commit to my intention?

_____

- Today I am grateful for?

_____

_____

- Today_____brought me joy.

DAILY INTENTION

Date: /   /

Questions to ask yourself today

- What do I need today?
- What is my why?
- What Inspires me?
- What is my heart's deepest desire?
- What do I need to do in order to succeed?
- What obstacles do I need to overcome if any and how will I do this?

Space for thoughts & feelings

Intention of the Day

Daily Reflection

- What have I done today to commit to my intention?

_____

- Today I am grateful for?

_____

_____

- Today_____brought me joy.

DAILY INTENTION

Date: /   /

Questions to ask yourself today

- What do I need today?
- What is my why?
- What Inspires me?
- What is my heart's deepest desire?
- What do I need to do in order to succeed?
- What obstacles do I need to overcome if any and how will I do this?

Space for thoughts & feelings

Intention of the Day

Daily Reflection

- What have I done today to commit to my intention?

_____

- Today I am grateful for?

_____

_____

- Today_____brought me joy.

DAILY INTENTION

Date: /   /

Questions to ask yourself today

- What do I need today?
- What is my why?
- What Inspires me?
- What is my heart's deepest desire?
- What do I need to do in order to succeed?
- What obstacles do I need to overcome if any and how will I do this?

Space for thoughts & feelings

Intention of the Day

Daily Reflection

- What have I done today to commit to my intention?

_____

- Today I am grateful for?

_____

_____

- Today_____brought me joy.

Date: /   /

Questions to ask yourself today

- What do I need today?
- What is my why?
- What Inspires me?
- What is my heart's deepest desire?
- What do I need to do in order to succeed?
- What obstacles do I need to overcome if any and how will I do this?

Space for thoughts & feelings

Intention of the Day

Daily Reflection

- What have I done today to commit to my intention?

_____

- Today I am grateful for?

_____

_____

- Today_____brought me joy.

Date: /   /

Questions to ask yourself today

- What do I need today?
- What is my why?
- What Inspires me?
- What is my heart's deepest desire?
- What do I need to do in order to succeed?
- What obstacles do I need to overcome if any and how will I do this?

Space for thoughts & feelings

Intention of the Day

Daily Reflection

- What have I done today to commit to my intention?

_____

- Today I am grateful for?

_____

_____

- Today_____brought me joy.

DAILY INTENTION

Date: /   /

Questions to ask yourself today

- What do I need today?
- What is my why?
- What Inspires me?
- What is my heart's deepest desire?
- What do I need to do in order to succeed?
- What obstacles do I need to overcome if any and how will I do this?

Space for thoughts & feelings

Intention of the Day

Daily Reflection

- What have I done today to commit to my intention?

_____

- Today I am grateful for?

_____

_____

- Today_____brought me joy.

DAILY INTENTION

Date: /   /

Questions to ask yourself today

- What do I need today?
- What is my why?
- What Inspires me?
- What is my heart's deepest desire?
- What do I need to do in order to succeed?
- What obstacles do I need to overcome if any and how will I do this?

> *Space for thoughts & feelings*

Intention of the Day

Daily Reflection

- What have I done today to commit to my intention?

_____

- Today I am grateful for?

_____

_____

- Today_____brought me joy.

DAILY INTENTION

Date: /   /

Questions to ask yourself today

- What do I need today?
- What is my why?
- What Inspires me?
- What is my heart's deepest desire?
- What do I need to do in order to succeed?
- What obstacles do I need to overcome if any and how will I do this?

Space for thoughts & feelings

Intention of the Day

Daily Reflection

- What have I done today to commit to my intention?

_____

- Today I am grateful for?

_____

_____

- Today_____brought me joy.

DAILY INTENTION

Date: /   /

Questions to ask yourself today

- What do I need today?
- What is my why?
- What Inspires me?
- What is my heart's deepest desire?
- What do I need to do in order to succeed?
- What obstacles do I need to overcome if any and how will I do this?

Space for thoughts & feelings

Intention of the Day

Daily Reflection

- What have I done today to commit to my intention?

_____

- Today I am grateful for?

_____

_____

- Today_____brought me joy.

DAILY INTENTION

Date: /   /

Questions to ask yourself today

- What do I need today?
- What is my why?
- What Inspires me?
- What is my heart's deepest desire?
- What do I need to do in order to succeed?
- What obstacles do I need to overcome if any and how will I do this?

> *Space for thoughts & feelings*

Intention of the Day

Daily Reflection

- What have I done today to commit to my intention?

_____

- Today I am grateful for?

_____

_____

- Today_____brought me joy.

DAILY INTENTION

Date: /   /

Questions to ask yourself today

- What do I need today?
- What is my why?
- What Inspires me?
- What is my heart's deepest desire?
- What do I need to do in order to succeed?
- What obstacles do I need to overcome if any and how will I do this?

Space for thoughts & feelings

Intention of the Day

Daily Reflection

- What have I done today to commit to my intention?

_____

- Today I am grateful for?

_____

_____

- Today_____brought me joy.

DAILY INTENTION

Date: /   /

Questions to ask yourself today

- What do I need today?
- What is my why?
- What Inspires me?
- What is my heart's deepest desire?
- What do I need to do in order to succeed?
- What obstacles do I need to overcome if any and how will I do this?

Space for thoughts & feelings

Intention of the Day

Daily Reflection

- What have I done today to commit to my intention?

_____

- Today I am grateful for?

_____

_____

- Today_____brought me joy.

DAILY INTENTION

Date: /   /

Questions to ask yourself today

- What do I need today?
- What is my why?
- What Inspires me?
- What is my heart's deepest desire?
- What do I need to do in order to succeed?
- What obstacles do I need to overcome if any and how will I do this?

Space for thoughts & feelings

Intention of the Day

Daily Reflection

- What have I done today to commit to my intention?

_____

- Today I am grateful for?

_____

_____

- Today_____brought me joy.

DAILY INTENTION

Date: /   /

Questions to ask yourself today

- What do I need today?
- What is my why?
- What Inspires me?
- What is my heart's deepest desire?
- What do I need to do in order to succeed?
- What obstacles do I need to overcome if any and how will I do this?

Space for thoughts & feelings

Intention of the Day

Daily Reflection

- What have I done today to commit to my intention?

_____

- Today I am grateful for?

_____

_____

- Today_____brought me joy.

DAILY INTENTION

Date: /   /

Questions to ask yourself today

- What do I need today?
- What is my why?
- What Inspires me?
- What is my heart's deepest desire?
- What do I need to do in order to succeed?
- What obstacles do I need to overcome if any and how will I do this?

Space for thoughts & feelings

Intention of the Day

Daily Reflection

- What have I done today to commit to my intention?

_____

- Today I am grateful for?

_____

_____

- Today_____brought me joy.

DAILY INTENTION

Date: /   /

Questions to ask yourself today

- What do I need today?
- What is my why?
- What Inspires me?
- What is my heart's deepest desire?
- What do I need to do in order to succeed?
- What obstacles do I need to overcome if any and how will I do this?

Space for thoughts & feelings

Intention of the Day

Daily Reflection

- What have I done today to commit to my intention?

_____

- Today I am grateful for?

_____
_____

- Today_____brought me joy.

DAILY INTENTION

Date: /   /

Questions to ask yourself today

- What do I need today?
- What is my why?
- What Inspires me?
- What is my heart's deepest desire?
- What do I need to do in order to succeed?
- What obstacles do I need to overcome if any and how will I do this?

Space for thoughts & feelings

Intention of the Day

Daily Reflection

- What have I done today to commit to my intention?

_____

- Today I am grateful for?

_____

_____

- Today_____brought me joy.

DAILY INTENTION

Date: /   /

Questions to ask yourself today

- What do I need today?
- What is my why?
- What Inspires me?
- What is my heart's deepest desire?
- What do I need to do in order to succeed?
- What obstacles do I need to overcome if any and how will I do this?

Space for thoughts & feelings

Intention of the Day

Daily Reflection

- What have I done today to commit to my intention?

_____

- Today I am grateful for?

_____

_____

- Today_____brought me joy.

DAILY INTENTION

Date: /   /

Questions to ask yourself today

- What do I need today?
- What is my why?
- What Inspires me?
- What is my heart's deepest desire?
- What do I need to do in order to succeed?
- What obstacles do I need to overcome if any and how will I do this?

> *Space for thoughts & feelings*

Intention of the Day

Daily Reflection

- What have I done today to commit to my intention?

_____

- Today I am grateful for?

_____

_____

- Today_____brought me joy.

DAILY INTENTION

Date: /   /

Questions to ask yourself today

- What do I need today?
- What is my why?
- What Inspires me?
- What is my heart's deepest desire?
- What do I need to do in order to succeed?
- What obstacles do I need to overcome if any and how will I do this?

Space for thoughts & feelings

Intention of the Day

Daily Reflection

- What have I done today to commit to my intention?

_____

- Today I am grateful for?

_____

_____

- Today_____brought me joy.

DAILY INTENTION

Date: /   /

Questions to ask yourself today

- What do I need today?
- What is my why?
- What Inspires me?
- What is my heart's deepest desire?
- What do I need to do in order to succeed?
- What obstacles do I need to overcome if any and how will I do this?

Space for thoughts & feelings

Intention of the Day

Daily Reflection

- What have I done today to commit to my intention?

_____

- Today I am grateful for?

_____

_____

- Today_____brought me joy.

DAILY INTENTION

Date: /   /

Questions to ask yourself today

- What do I need today?
- What is my why?
- What Inspires me?
- What is my heart's deepest desire?
- What do I need to do in order to succeed?
- What obstacles do I need to overcome if any and how will I do this?

Space for thoughts & feelings

Intention of the Day

Daily Reflection

- What have I done today to commit to my intention?

_____

- Today I am grateful for?

_____

_____

- Today_____brought me joy.

Date: /   /

Questions to ask yourself today

- What do I need today?
- What is my why?
- What Inspires me?
- What is my heart's deepest desire?
- What do I need to do in order to succeed?
- What obstacles do I need to overcome if any and how will I do this?

Space for thoughts & feelings

Intention of the Day

Daily Reflection

- What have I done today to commit to my intention?

_____

- Today I am grateful for?

_____

_____

- Today_____brought me joy.

DAILY INTENTION

Date: /   /

Questions to ask yourself today

- What do I need today?
- What is my why?
- What Inspires me?
- What is my heart's deepest desire?
- What do I need to do in order to succeed?
- What obstacles do I need to overcome if any and how will I do this?

> *Space for thoughts & feelings*

Intention of the Day

Daily Reflection

- What have I done today to commit to my intention?

_____

- Today I am grateful for?

_____

_____

- Today_____brought me joy.

DAILY INTENTION

Date: /   /

Questions to ask yourself today

- What do I need today?
- What is my why?
- What Inspires me?
- What is my heart's deepest desire?
- What do I need to do in order to succeed?
- What obstacles do I need to overcome if any and how will I do this?

> *Space for thoughts & feelings*

Intention of the Day

Daily Reflection

- What have I done today to commit to my intention?

_____

- Today I am grateful for?

_____

_____

- Today_____brought me joy.

DAILY INTENTION

Date:　　　/　　　/

Questions to ask yourself today

- What do I need today?
- What is my why?
- What Inspires me?
- What is my heart's deepest desire?
- What do I need to do in order to succeed?
- What obstacles do I need to overcome if any and how will I do this?

Space for thoughts & feelings

Intention of the Day

Daily Reflection

- What have I done today to commit to my intention?

_____

- Today I am grateful for?

_____

_____

- Today_____brought me joy.

DAILY INTENTION

Date: /   /

Questions to ask yourself today

- What do I need today?
- What is my why?
- What Inspires me?
- What is my heart's deepest desire?
- What do I need to do in order to succeed?
- What obstacles do I need to overcome if any and how will I do this?

> *Space for thoughts & feelings*

Intention of the Day

Daily Reflection

- What have I done today to commit to my intention?

_____

- Today I am grateful for?

_____

_____

- Today_____brought me joy.

DAILY INTENTION

Date: /   /

Questions to ask yourself today

- What do I need today?
- What is my why?
- What Inspires me?
- What is my heart's deepest desire?
- What do I need to do in order to succeed?
- What obstacles do I need to overcome if any and how will I do this?

Space for thoughts & feelings

Intention of the Day

Daily Reflection

- What have I done today to commit to my intention?

_____

- Today I am grateful for?

_____

_____

- Today_____brought me joy.

DAILY INTENTION

Date: /   /

Questions to ask yourself today

- What do I need today?
- What is my why?
- What Inspires me?
- What is my heart's deepest desire?
- What do I need to do in order to succeed?
- What obstacles do I need to overcome if any and how will I do this?

Space for thoughts & feelings

Intention of the Day

Daily Reflection

- What have I done today to commit to my intention?

_____

- Today I am grateful for?

_____

_____

- Today_____brought me joy.

DAILY INTENTION

Date: /   /

Questions to ask yourself today

- What do I need today?
- What is my why?
- What Inspires me?
- What is my heart's deepest desire?
- What do I need to do in order to succeed?
- What obstacles do I need to overcome if any and how will I do this?

Space for thoughts & feelings

Intention of the Day

Daily Reflection

- What have I done today to commit to my intention?

_____

- Today I am grateful for?

_____

_____

- Today_____brought me joy.

DAILY INTENTION

Date: /   /

Questions to ask yourself today

- What do I need today?
- What is my why?
- What Inspires me?
- What is my heart's deepest desire?
- What do I need to do in order to succeed?
- What obstacles do I need to overcome if any and how will I do this?

Space for thoughts & feelings

Intention of the Day

Daily Reflection

- What have I done today to commit to my intention?

_____

- Today I am grateful for?

_____

_____

- Today_____brought me joy.

DAILY INTENTION

Date: /   /

Questions to ask yourself today

- What do I need today?
- What is my why?
- What Inspires me?
- What is my heart's deepest desire?
- What do I need to do in order to succeed?
- What obstacles do I need to overcome if any and how will I do this?

Space for thoughts & feelings

Intention of the Day

Daily Reflection

- What have I done today to commit to my intention?

_____

- Today I am grateful for?

_____

_____

- Today_____brought me joy.

Date: /   /

Questions to ask yourself today

- What do I need today?
- What is my why?
- What Inspires me?
- What is my heart's deepest desire?
- What do I need to do in order to succeed?
- What obstacles do I need to overcome if any and how will I do this?

Space for thoughts & feelings

Intention of the Day

Daily Reflection

- What have I done today to commit to my intention?

_____

- Today I am grateful for?

_____

_____

- Today_____brought me joy.

DAILY INTENTION

Date: /   /

Questions to ask yourself today

- What do I need today?
- What is my why?
- What Inspires me?
- What is my heart's deepest desire?
- What do I need to do in order to succeed?
- What obstacles do I need to overcome if any and how will I do this?

> *Space for thoughts & feelings*

Intention of the Day

Daily Reflection

- What have I done today to commit to my intention?

_____

- Today I am grateful for?

_____

_____

- Today_____brought me joy.

DAILY INTENTION

Date: /   /

Questions to ask yourself today

- What do I need today?
- What is my why?
- What Inspires me?
- What is my heart's deepest desire?
- What do I need to do in order to succeed?
- What obstacles do I need to overcome if any and how will I do this?

Space for thoughts & feelings

Intention of the Day

Daily Reflection

- What have I done today to commit to my intention?

_____

- Today I am grateful for?

_____

_____

- Today_____brought me joy.

DAILY INTENTION

Date: /   /

Questions to ask yourself today

- What do I need today?
- What is my why?
- What Inspires me?
- What is my heart's deepest desire?
- What do I need to do in order to succeed?
- What obstacles do I need to overcome if any and how will I do this?

Space for thoughts & feelings

Intention of the Day

Daily Reflection

- What have I done today to commit to my intention?

_____

- Today I am grateful for?

_____

_____

- Today_____brought me joy.

Date: /   /

Questions to ask yourself today

- What do I need today?
- What is my why?
- What Inspires me?
- What is my heart's deepest desire?
- What do I need to do in order to succeed?
- What obstacles do I need to overcome if any and how will I do this?

Space for thoughts & feelings

Intention of the Day

Daily Reflection

- What have I done today to commit to my intention?

_____

- Today I am grateful for?

_____

_____

- Today_____brought me joy.

DAILY INTENTION

Date: /   /

Questions to ask yourself today

- What do I need today?
- What is my why?
- What Inspires me?
- What is my heart's deepest desire?
- What do I need to do in order to succeed?
- What obstacles do I need to overcome if any and how will I do this?

Space for thoughts & feelings

Intention of the Day

Daily Reflection

- What have I done today to commit to my intention?

_____

- Today I am grateful for?

_____

_____

- Today_____brought me joy.

DAILY INTENTION

Date: /   /

Questions to ask yourself today

- What do I need today?
- What is my why?
- What Inspires me?
- What is my heart's deepest desire?
- What do I need to do in order to succeed?
- What obstacles do I need to overcome if any and how will I do this?

Space for thoughts & feelings

Intention of the Day

Daily Reflection

- What have I done today to commit to my intention?

_____

- Today I am grateful for?

_____

_____

- Today_____brought me joy.

DAILY INTENTION

Date: /   /

Questions to ask yourself today

- What do I need today?
- What is my why?
- What Inspires me?
- What is my heart's deepest desire?
- What do I need to do in order to succeed?
- What obstacles do I need to overcome if any and how will I do this?

Space for thoughts & feelings

Intention of the Day

Daily Reflection

- What have I done today to commit to my intention?

_____

- Today I am grateful for?

_____

_____

- Today_____brought me joy.

DAILY INTENTION

Date: /   /

Questions to ask yourself today

- What do I need today?
- What is my why?
- What Inspires me?
- What is my heart's deepest desire?
- What do I need to do in order to succeed?
- What obstacles do I need to overcome if any and how will I do this?

Space for thoughts & feelings

Intention of the Day

Daily Reflection

- What have I done today to commit to my intention?

_____

- Today I am grateful for?

_____

_____

- Today_____brought me joy.

DAILY INTENTION

Date: /   /

Questions to ask yourself today

- What do I need today?
- What is my why?
- What Inspires me?
- What is my heart's deepest desire?
- What do I need to do in order to succeed?
- What obstacles do I need to overcome if any and how will I do this?

Space for thoughts & feelings

Intention of the Day

Daily Reflection

- What have I done today to commit to my intention?

_____

- Today I am grateful for?

_____

_____

- Today_____brought me joy.

DAILY INTENTION

Date: /   /

Questions to ask yourself today

- What do I need today?
- What is my why?
- What Inspires me?
- What is my heart's deepest desire?
- What do I need to do in order to succeed?
- What obstacles do I need to overcome if any and how will I do this?

Space for thoughts & feelings

Intention of the Day

Daily Reflection

- What have I done today to commit to my intention?

_____

- Today I am grateful for?

_____

_____

- Today_____brought me joy.

DAILY INTENTION

Date: /   /

Questions to ask yourself today

- What do I need today?
- What is my why?
- What Inspires me?
- What is my heart's deepest desire?
- What do I need to do in order to succeed?
- What obstacles do I need to overcome if any and how will I do this?

Space for thoughts & feelings

Intention of the Day

Daily Reflection

- What have I done today to commit to my intention?

_____

- Today I am grateful for?

_____

_____

- Today_____brought me joy.

DAILY INTENTION

Date: /   /

Questions to ask yourself today

- What do I need today?
- What is my why?
- What Inspires me?
- What is my heart's deepest desire?
- What do I need to do in order to succeed?
- What obstacles do I need to overcome if any and how will I do this?

Space for thoughts & feelings

Intention of the Day

Daily Reflection

- What have I done today to commit to my intention?

_____

- Today I am grateful for?

_____

_____

- Today_____brought me joy.

DAILY INTENTION

Date: /   /

Questions to ask yourself today

- What do I need today?
- What is my why?
- What Inspires me?
- What is my heart's deepest desire?
- What do I need to do in order to succeed?
- What obstacles do I need to overcome if any and how will I do this?

Space for thoughts & feelings

Intention of the Day

Daily Reflection

- What have I done today to commit to my intention?

_____

- Today I am grateful for?

_____

_____

- Today_____brought me joy.

Date: /   /

Questions to ask yourself today

- What do I need today?
- What is my why?
- What Inspires me?
- What is my heart's deepest desire?
- What do I need to do in order to succeed?
- What obstacles do I need to overcome if any and how will I do this?

> *Space for thoughts & feelings*

Intention of the Day

Daily Reflection

- What have I done today to commit to my intention?

_____

- Today I am grateful for?

_____

_____

- Today_____brought me joy.

DAILY INTENTION

Date: /   /

Questions to ask yourself today

- What do I need today?
- What is my why?
- What Inspires me?
- What is my heart's deepest desire?
- What do I need to do in order to succeed?
- What obstacles do I need to overcome if any and how will I do this?

Space for thoughts & feelings

Intention of the Day

Daily Reflection

- What have I done today to commit to my intention?

_____

- Today I am grateful for?

_____

_____

- Today_____brought me joy.

DAILY INTENTION

Date: /   /

Questions to ask yourself today

- What do I need today?
- What is my why?
- What Inspires me?
- What is my heart's deepest desire?
- What do I need to do in order to succeed?
- What obstacles do I need to overcome if any and how will I do this?

Space for thoughts & feelings

Intention of the Day

Daily Reflection

- What have I done today to commit to my intention?

_____

- Today I am grateful for?

_____

_____

- Today_____brought me joy.

DAILY INTENTION

Date: /   /

Questions to ask yourself today

- What do I need today?
- What is my why?
- What Inspires me?
- What is my heart's deepest desire?
- What do I need to do in order to succeed?
- What obstacles do I need to overcome if any and how will I do this?

Space for thoughts & feelings

Intention of the Day

Daily Reflection

- What have I done today to commit to my intention?

_____

- Today I am grateful for?

_____

_____

- Today_____brought me joy.

DAILY INTENTION

Date: /   /

Questions to ask yourself today

- What do I need today?
- What is my why?
- What Inspires me?
- What is my heart's deepest desire?
- What do I need to do in order to succeed?
- What obstacles do I need to overcome if any and how will I do this?

> *Space for thoughts & feelings*

Intention of the Day

Daily Reflection

- What have I done today to commit to my intention?

_____

- Today I am grateful for?

_____

_____

- Today_____brought me joy.

DAILY INTENTION

Date: /   /

Questions to ask yourself today

- What do I need today?
- What is my why?
- What Inspires me?
- What is my heart's deepest desire?
- What do I need to do in order to succeed?
- What obstacles do I need to overcome if any and how will I do this?

Space for thoughts & feelings

Intention of the Day

Daily Reflection

- What have I done today to commit to my intention?

_____

- Today I am grateful for?

_____

_____

- Today_____brought me joy.

DAILY INTENTION

Date: /   /

Questions to ask yourself today

- What do I need today?
- What is my why?
- What Inspires me?
- What is my heart's deepest desire?
- What do I need to do in order to succeed?
- What obstacles do I need to overcome if any and how will I do this?

> *Space for thoughts & feelings*

Intention of the Day

Daily Reflection

- What have I done today to commit to my intention?

_____

- Today I am grateful for?

_____

_____

- Today_____brought me joy.

Date: /   /

Questions to ask yourself today

- What do I need today?
- What is my why?
- What Inspires me?
- What is my heart's deepest desire?
- What do I need to do in order to succeed?
- What obstacles do I need to overcome if any and how will I do this?

Space for thoughts & feelings

Intention of the Day

Daily Reflection

- What have I done today to commit to my intention?

_____

- Today I am grateful for?

_____

_____

- Today_____brought me joy.

DAILY INTENTION

Date: /   /

Questions to ask yourself today

- What do I need today?
- What is my why?
- What Inspires me?
- What is my heart's deepest desire?
- What do I need to do in order to succeed?
- What obstacles do I need to overcome if any and how will I do this?

Space for thoughts & feelings

Intention of the Day

Daily Reflection

- What have I done today to commit to my intention?

_____

- Today I am grateful for?

_____

_____

- Today_____brought me joy.

DAILY INTENTION

Date:　　　/　　　/

Questions to ask yourself today

- What do I need today?
- What is my why?
- What Inspires me?
- What is my heart's deepest desire?
- What do I need to do in order to succeed?
- What obstacles do I need to overcome if any and how will I do this?

Space for thoughts & feelings

Intention of the Day

Daily Reflection

- What have I done today to commit to my intention?

_____

- Today I am grateful for?

_____

_____

- Today_____brought me joy.

Date: /   /

Questions to ask yourself today

- What do I need today?
- What is my why?
- What Inspires me?
- What is my heart's deepest desire?
- What do I need to do in order to succeed?
- What obstacles do I need to overcome if any and how will I do this?

Space for thoughts & feelings

Intention of the Day

Daily Reflection

- What have I done today to commit to my intention?

_____

- Today I am grateful for?

_____

_____

- Today_____brought me joy.

DAILY INTENTION

Date: /   /

Questions to ask yourself today

- What do I need today?
- What is my why?
- What Inspires me?
- What is my heart's deepest desire?
- What do I need to do in order to succeed?
- What obstacles do I need to overcome if any and how will I do this?

Space for thoughts & feelings

Intention of the Day

Daily Reflection

- What have I done today to commit to my intention?

_____

- Today I am grateful for?

_____

_____

- Today_____brought me joy.

DAILY INTENTION

Date: /   /

Questions to ask yourself today

- What do I need today?
- What is my why?
- What Inspires me?
- What is my heart's deepest desire?
- What do I need to do in order to succeed?
- What obstacles do I need to overcome if any and how will I do this?

Space for thoughts & feelings

Intention of the Day

Daily Reflection

- What have I done today to commit to my intention?

_____

- Today I am grateful for?

_____

_____

- Today_____brought me joy.

DAILY INTENTION

Date: /   /

Questions to ask yourself today

- What do I need today?
- What is my why?
- What Inspires me?
- What is my heart's deepest desire?
- What do I need to do in order to succeed?
- What obstacles do I need to overcome if any and how will I do this?

Space for thoughts & feelings

Intention of the Day

Daily Reflection

- What have I done today to commit to my intention?

_____

- Today I am grateful for?

_____

_____

- Today_____brought me joy.

DAILY INTENTION

Date: /   /

Questions to ask yourself today

- What do I need today?
- What is my why?
- What Inspires me?
- What is my heart's deepest desire?
- What do I need to do in order to succeed?
- What obstacles do I need to overcome if any and how will I do this?

Space for thoughts & feelings

Intention of the Day

Daily Reflection

- What have I done today to commit to my intention?

_____

- Today I am grateful for?

_____

_____

- Today_____brought me joy.

DAILY INTENTION

Date: /   /

Questions to ask yourself today

- What do I need today?
- What is my why?
- What Inspires me?
- What is my heart's deepest desire?
- What do I need to do in order to succeed?
- What obstacles do I need to overcome if any and how will I do this?

Space for thoughts & feelings

Intention of the Day

Daily Reflection

- What have I done today to commit to my intention?

_____

- Today I am grateful for?

_____

_____

- Today_____brought me joy.

DAILY INTENTION

Date: /   /

Questions to ask yourself today

- What do I need today?
- What is my why?
- What Inspires me?
- What is my heart's deepest desire?
- What do I need to do in order to succeed?
- What obstacles do I need to overcome if any and how will I do this?

Space for thoughts & feelings

Intention of the Day

Daily Reflection

- What have I done today to commit to my intention?

_____

- Today I am grateful for?

_____

_____

- Today_____brought me joy.

DAILY INTENTION

Date: /   /

Questions to ask yourself today

- What do I need today?
- What is my why?
- What Inspires me?
- What is my heart's deepest desire?
- What do I need to do in order to succeed?
- What obstacles do I need to overcome if any and how will I do this?

Space for thoughts & feelings

Intention of the Day

Daily Reflection

- What have I done today to commit to my intention?

_____

- Today I am grateful for?

_____

_____

- Today_____brought me joy.

DAILY INTENTION

Date: /   /

Questions to ask yourself today

- What do I need today?
- What is my why?
- What Inspires me?
- What is my heart's deepest desire?
- What do I need to do in order to succeed?
- What obstacles do I need to overcome if any and how will I do this?

Space for thoughts & feelings

Intention of the Day

Daily Reflection

- What have I done today to commit to my intention?

_____

- Today I am grateful for?

_____

_____

- Today_____brought me joy.

DAILY INTENTION

Date: /   /

Questions to ask yourself today

- What do I need today?
- What is my why?
- What Inspires me?
- What is my heart's deepest desire?
- What do I need to do in order to succeed?
- What obstacles do I need to overcome if any and how will I do this?

Space for thoughts & feelings

Intention of the Day

Daily Reflection

- What have I done today to commit to my intention?

_____

- Today I am grateful for?

_____

_____

- Today_____brought me joy.

DAILY INTENTION

Date: /   /

Questions to ask yourself today

- What do I need today?
- What is my why?
- What Inspires me?
- What is my heart's deepest desire?
- What do I need to do in order to succeed?
- What obstacles do I need to overcome if any and how will I do this?

Space for thoughts & feelings

Intention of the Day

Daily Reflection

- What have I done today to commit to my intention?

_____

- Today I am grateful for?

_____

_____

- Today_____brought me joy.

DAILY INTENTION

Date: /   /

Questions to ask yourself today

- What do I need today?
- What is my why?
- What Inspires me?
- What is my heart's deepest desire?
- What do I need to do in order to succeed?
- What obstacles do I need to overcome if any and how will I do this?

Space for thoughts & feelings

Intention of the Day

Daily Reflection

- What have I done today to commit to my intention?

_____

- Today I am grateful for?

_____

_____

- Today_____brought me joy.

DAILY INTENTION

Date: /   /

Questions to ask yourself today

- What do I need today?
- What is my why?
- What Inspires me?
- What is my heart's deepest desire?
- What do I need to do in order to succeed?
- What obstacles do I need to overcome if any and how will I do this?

Space for thoughts & feelings

Intention of the Day

Daily Reflection

- What have I done today to commit to my intention?

_____

- Today I am grateful for?

_____

_____

- Today_____brought me joy.

DAILY INTENTION

Date: /   /

Questions to ask yourself today

- What do I need today?
- What is my why?
- What Inspires me?
- What is my heart's deepest desire?
- What do I need to do in order to succeed?
- What obstacles do I need to overcome if any and how will I do this?

Space for thoughts & feelings

Intention of the Day

Daily Reflection

- What have I done today to commit to my intention?

_____

- Today I am grateful for?

_____

_____

- Today_____brought me joy.

DAILY INTENTION

Date: /   /

Questions to ask yourself today

- What do I need today?
- What is my why?
- What Inspires me?
- What is my heart's deepest desire?
- What do I need to do in order to succeed?
- What obstacles do I need to overcome if any and how will I do this?

Space for thoughts & feelings

Intention of the Day

Daily Reflection

- What have I done today to commit to my intention?

_____

- Today I am grateful for?

_____

_____

- Today_____brought me joy.

DAILY INTENTION

Date: /   /

Questions to ask yourself today

- What do I need today?
- What is my why?
- What Inspires me?
- What is my heart's deepest desire?
- What do I need to do in order to succeed?
- What obstacles do I need to overcome if any and how will I do this?

Space for thoughts & feelings

Intention of the Day

Daily Reflection

- What have I done today to commit to my intention?

_____

- Today I am grateful for?

_____

_____

- Today_____brought me joy.

DAILY INTENTION

Date: /   /

Questions to ask yourself today

- What do I need today?
- What is my why?
- What Inspires me?
- What is my heart's deepest desire?
- What do I need to do in order to succeed?
- What obstacles do I need to overcome if any and how will I do this?

Space for thoughts & feelings

Intention of the Day

Daily Reflection

- What have I done today to commit to my intention?

_____

- Today I am grateful for?

_____

_____

- Today_____brought me joy.

DAILY INTENTION

Date: /   /

Questions to ask yourself today

- What do I need today?
- What is my why?
- What Inspires me?
- What is my heart's deepest desire?
- What do I need to do in order to succeed?
- What obstacles do I need to overcome if any and how will I do this?

Space for thoughts & feelings

Intention of the Day

Daily Reflection

- What have I done today to commit to my intention?

_____

- Today I am grateful for?

_____

_____

- Today_____brought me joy.

DAILY INTENTION

Date: /   /

Questions to ask yourself today

- What do I need today?
- What is my why?
- What Inspires me?
- What is my heart's deepest desire?
- What do I need to do in order to succeed?
- What obstacles do I need to overcome if any and how will I do this?

> *Space for thoughts & feelings*

Intention of the Day

Daily Reflection

- What have I done today to commit to my intention?

_____

- Today I am grateful for?

_____

_____

- Today_____brought me joy.

DAILY INTENTION

Date: /   /

Questions to ask yourself today

- What do I need today?
- What is my why?
- What Inspires me?
- What is my heart's deepest desire?
- What do I need to do in order to succeed?
- What obstacles do I need to overcome if any and how will I do this?

Space for thoughts & feelings

Intention of the Day

Daily Reflection

- What have I done today to commit to my intention?

_____

- Today I am grateful for?

_____

_____

- Today_____brought me joy.

DAILY INTENTION

Date: /   /

Questions to ask yourself today

- What do I need today?
- What is my why?
- What Inspires me?
- What is my heart's deepest desire?
- What do I need to do in order to succeed?
- What obstacles do I need to overcome if any and how will I do this?

> *Space for thoughts & feelings*

Intention of the Day

Daily Reflection

- What have I done today to commit to my intention?

_____

- Today I am grateful for?

_____

_____

- Today_____brought me joy.

DAILY INTENTION

Date: /   /

Questions to ask yourself today

- What do I need today?
- What is my why?
- What Inspires me?
- What is my heart's deepest desire?
- What do I need to do in order to succeed?
- What obstacles do I need to overcome if any and how will I do this?

Space for thoughts & feelings

Intention of the Day

Daily Reflection

- What have I done today to commit to my intention?

_____

- Today I am grateful for?

_____

_____

- Today_____brought me joy.

Date: /   /

Questions to ask yourself today

- What do I need today?
- What is my why?
- What Inspires me?
- What is my heart's deepest desire?
- What do I need to do in order to succeed?
- What obstacles do I need to overcome if any and how will I do this?

> *Space for thoughts & feelings*

Intention of the Day

Daily Reflection

- What have I done today to commit to my intention?

_____

- Today I am grateful for?

_____

_____

- Today_____brought me joy.

DAILY INTENTION

Date: /   /

Questions to ask yourself today

- What do I need today?
- What is my why?
- What Inspires me?
- What is my heart's deepest desire?
- What do I need to do in order to succeed?
- What obstacles do I need to overcome if any and how will I do this?

Space for thoughts & feelings

Intention of the Day

Daily Reflection

- What have I done today to commit to my intention?

_____

- Today I am grateful for?

_____

_____

- Today_____brought me joy.

DAILY INTENTION

Date: /   /

Questions to ask yourself today

- What do I need today?
- What is my why?
- What Inspires me?
- What is my heart's deepest desire?
- What do I need to do in order to succeed?
- What obstacles do I need to overcome if any and how will I do this?

> *Space for thoughts & feelings*

> **Intention of the Day**

Daily Reflection

- What have I done today to commit to my intention?

_____

- Today I am grateful for?

_____

_____

- Today_____brought me joy.

DAILY INTENTION

Date: /   /

Questions to ask yourself today

- What do I need today?
- What is my why?
- What Inspires me?
- What is my heart's deepest desire?
- What do I need to do in order to succeed?
- What obstacles do I need to overcome if any and how will I do this?

Space for thoughts & feelings

Intention of the Day

Daily Reflection

- What have I done today to commit to my intention?

- Today I am grateful for?

- Today_____brought me joy.

DAILY INTENTION

Date: /   /

Questions to ask yourself today

- What do I need today?
- What is my why?
- What Inspires me?
- What is my heart's deepest desire?
- What do I need to do in order to succeed?
- What obstacles do I need to overcome if any and how will I do this?

Space for thoughts & feelings

Intention of the Day

Daily Reflection

- What have I done today to commit to my intention?

_____

- Today I am grateful for?

_____

_____

- Today_____brought me joy.

Date: /   /

Questions to ask yourself today

- What do I need today?
- What is my why?
- What Inspires me?
- What is my heart's deepest desire?
- What do I need to do in order to succeed?
- What obstacles do I need to overcome if any and how will I do this?

Space for thoughts & feelings

Intention of the Day

Daily Reflection

- What have I done today to commit to my intention?

_____

- Today I am grateful for?

_____

_____

- Today_____brought me joy.

DAILY INTENTION

Date: /   /

Questions to ask yourself today

- What do I need today?
- What is my why?
- What Inspires me?
- What is my heart's deepest desire?
- What do I need to do in order to succeed?
- What obstacles do I need to overcome if any and how will I do this?

Space for thoughts & feelings

Intention of the Day

Daily Reflection

- What have I done today to commit to my intention?

_____

- Today I am grateful for?

_____

_____

- Today_____brought me joy.

DAILY INTENTION

Date: /   /

Questions to ask yourself today

- What do I need today?
- What is my why?
- What Inspires me?
- What is my heart's deepest desire?
- What do I need to do in order to succeed?
- What obstacles do I need to overcome if any and how will I do this?

Space for thoughts & feelings

Intention of the Day

Daily Reflection

- What have I done today to commit to my intention?

_____

- Today I am grateful for?

_____

_____

- Today_____brought me joy.

DAILY INTENTION

Date: /   /

Questions to ask yourself today

- What do I need today?
- What is my why?
- What Inspires me?
- What is my heart's deepest desire?
- What do I need to do in order to succeed?
- What obstacles do I need to overcome if any and how will I do this?

Space for thoughts & feelings

Intention of the Day

Daily Reflection

- What have I done today to commit to my intention?

_____

- Today I am grateful for?

_____

_____

- Today_____brought me joy.

DAILY INTENTION

Date: /   /

Questions to ask yourself today

- What do I need today?
- What is my why?
- What Inspires me?
- What is my heart's deepest desire?
- What do I need to do in order to succeed?
- What obstacles do I need to overcome if any and how will I do this?

Space for thoughts & feelings

Intention of the Day

Daily Reflection

- What have I done today to commit to my intention?

_____

- Today I am grateful for?

_____

_____

- Today_____brought me joy.

DAILY INTENTION

Date: /   /

Questions to ask yourself today

- What do I need today?
- What is my why?
- What Inspires me?
- What is my heart's deepest desire?
- What do I need to do in order to succeed?
- What obstacles do I need to overcome if any and how will I do this?

Space for thoughts & feelings

Intention of the Day

Daily Reflection

- What have I done today to commit to my intention?

_____

- Today I am grateful for?

_____

_____

- Today_____brought me joy.

DAILY INTENTION

Date: /   /

Questions to ask yourself today

- What do I need today?
- What is my why?
- What Inspires me?
- What is my heart's deepest desire?
- What do I need to do in order to succeed?
- What obstacles do I need to overcome if any and how will I do this?

Space for thoughts & feelings

Intention of the Day

Daily Reflection

- What have I done today to commit to my intention?

_____

- Today I am grateful for?

_____

_____

- Today_____brought me joy.

DAILY INTENTION

Date: /   /

Questions to ask yourself today

- What do I need today?
- What is my why?
- What Inspires me?
- What is my heart's deepest desire?
- What do I need to do in order to succeed?
- What obstacles do I need to overcome if any and how will I do this?

> *Space for thoughts & feelings*

Intention of the Day

Daily Reflection

- What have I done today to commit to my intention?

_____

- Today I am grateful for?

_____

_____

- Today_____brought me joy.

DAILY INTENTION

Date: /   /

Questions to ask yourself today

- What do I need today?
- What is my why?
- What Inspires me?
- What is my heart's deepest desire?
- What do I need to do in order to succeed?
- What obstacles do I need to overcome if any and how will I do this?

Space for thoughts & feelings

Intention of the Day

Daily Reflection

- What have I done today to commit to my intention?

_____

- Today I am grateful for?

_____

_____

- Today_____brought me joy.

DAILY INTENTION

Date: /   /

Questions to ask yourself today

- What do I need today?
- What is my why?
- What Inspires me?
- What is my heart's deepest desire?
- What do I need to do in order to succeed?
- What obstacles do I need to overcome if any and how will I do this?

> *Space for thoughts & feelings*

Intention of the Day

Daily Reflection

- What have I done today to commit to my intention?

_____

- Today I am grateful for?

_____

_____

- Today_____brought me joy.

DAILY INTENTION

Date: /   /

Questions to ask yourself today

- What do I need today?
- What is my why?
- What Inspires me?
- What is my heart's deepest desire?
- What do I need to do in order to succeed?
- What obstacles do I need to overcome if any and how will I do this?

> Space for thoughts & feelings

Intention of the Day

Daily Reflection

- What have I done today to commit to my intention?

_____

- Today I am grateful for?

_____

_____

- Today_____brought me joy.

DAILY INTENTION

Date: /   /

Questions to ask yourself today

- What do I need today?
- What is my why?
- What Inspires me?
- What is my heart's deepest desire?
- What do I need to do in order to succeed?
- What obstacles do I need to overcome if any and how will I do this?

Space for thoughts & feelings

Intention of the Day

Daily Reflection

- What have I done today to commit to my intention?

_____

- Today I am grateful for?

_____

_____

- Today_____brought me joy.

DAILY INTENTION

Date: /   /

Questions to ask yourself today

- What do I need today?
- What is my why?
- What Inspires me?
- What is my heart's deepest desire?
- What do I need to do in order to succeed?
- What obstacles do I need to overcome if any and how will I do this?

Space for thoughts & feelings

Intention of the Day

Daily Reflection

- What have I done today to commit to my intention?

_____

- Today I am grateful for?

_____

_____

- Today_____brought me joy.

DAILY INTENTION

Date: /   /

Questions to ask yourself today

- What do I need today?
- What is my why?
- What Inspires me?
- What is my heart's deepest desire?
- What do I need to do in order to succeed?
- What obstacles do I need to overcome if any and how will I do this?

Space for thoughts & feelings

Intention of the Day

Daily Reflection

- What have I done today to commit to my intention?

_____

- Today I am grateful for?

_____

_____

- Today_____brought me joy.

DAILY INTENTION

Date: /   /

Questions to ask yourself today

- What do I need today?
- What is my why?
- What Inspires me?
- What is my heart's deepest desire?
- What do I need to do in order to succeed?
- What obstacles do I need to overcome if any and how will I do this?

Space for thoughts & feelings

Intention of the Day

Daily Reflection

- What have I done today to commit to my intention?

_____

- Today I am grateful for?

_____

_____

- Today_____brought me joy.

DAILY INTENTION

Date: /   /

Questions to ask yourself today

- What do I need today?
- What is my why?
- What Inspires me?
- What is my heart's deepest desire?
- What do I need to do in order to succeed?
- What obstacles do I need to overcome if any and how will I do this?

Space for thoughts & feelings

Intention of the Day

Daily Reflection

- What have I done today to commit to my intention?

_____

- Today I am grateful for?

_____

_____

- Today_____brought me joy.

DAILY INTENTION

Date: /   /

Questions to ask yourself today

- What do I need today?
- What is my why?
- What Inspires me?
- What is my heart's deepest desire?
- What do I need to do in order to succeed?
- What obstacles do I need to overcome if any and how will I do this?

Space for thoughts & feelings

Intention of the Day

Daily Reflection

- What have I done today to commit to my intention?

_____

- Today I am grateful for?

_____

_____

- Today_____brought me joy.

Date: /   /

Questions to ask yourself today

- What do I need today?
- What is my why?
- What Inspires me?
- What is my heart's deepest desire?
- What do I need to do in order to succeed?
- What obstacles do I need to overcome if any and how will I do this?

Space for thoughts & feelings

Intention of the Day

Daily Reflection

- What have I done today to commit to my intention?

_____

- Today I am grateful for?

_____

_____

- Today_____brought me joy.

DAILY INTENTION

Date: /   /

Questions to ask yourself today

- What do I need today?
- What is my why?
- What Inspires me?
- What is my heart's deepest desire?
- What do I need to do in order to succeed?
- What obstacles do I need to overcome if any and how will I do this?

Space for thoughts & feelings

Intention of the Day

Daily Reflection

- What have I done today to commit to my intention?

_____

- Today I am grateful for?

_____

_____

- Today_____brought me joy.

DAILY INTENTION

Date: / /

Questions to ask yourself today

- What do I need today?
- What is my why?
- What Inspires me?
- What is my heart's deepest desire?
- What do I need to do in order to succeed?
- What obstacles do I need to overcome if any and how will I do this?

Space for thoughts & feelings

Intention of the Day

Daily Reflection

- What have I done today to commit to my intention?

_____

- Today I am grateful for?

_____

_____

- Today_____brought me joy.

DAILY INTENTION

Date: /   /

Questions to ask yourself today

- What do I need today?
- What is my why?
- What Inspires me?
- What is my heart's deepest desire?
- What do I need to do in order to succeed?
- What obstacles do I need to overcome if any and how will I do this?

Space for thoughts & feelings

Intention of the Day

Daily Reflection

- What have I done today to commit to my intention?

_____

- Today I am grateful for?

_____

_____

- Today_____brought me joy.

DAILY INTENTION

Date: /   /

Questions to ask yourself today

- What do I need today?
- What is my why?
- What Inspires me?
- What is my heart's deepest desire?
- What do I need to do in order to succeed?
- What obstacles do I need to overcome if any and how will I do this?

Space for thoughts & feelings

Intention of the Day

Daily Reflection

- What have I done today to commit to my intention?

_____

- Today I am grateful for?

_____

_____

- Today_____brought me joy.

DAILY INTENTION

Date: /   /

Questions to ask yourself today

- What do I need today?
- What is my why?
- What Inspires me?
- What is my heart's deepest desire?
- What do I need to do in order to succeed?
- What obstacles do I need to overcome if any and how will I do this?

> *Space for thoughts & feelings*

Intention of the Day

Daily Reflection

- What have I done today to commit to my intention?

_____

- Today I am grateful for?

_____

_____

- Today_____brought me joy.

DAILY INTENTION

Date: /   /

Questions to ask yourself today

- What do I need today?
- What is my why?
- What Inspires me?
- What is my heart's deepest desire?
- What do I need to do in order to succeed?
- What obstacles do I need to overcome if any and how will I do this?

Space for thoughts & feelings

Intention of the Day

Daily Reflection

- What have I done today to commit to my intention?

_____

- Today I am grateful for?

_____

_____

- Today_____brought me joy.

Date: /   /

Questions to ask yourself today

- What do I need today?
- What is my why?
- What Inspires me?
- What is my heart's deepest desire?
- What do I need to do in order to succeed?
- What obstacles do I need to overcome if any and how will I do this?

Space for thoughts & feelings

Intention of the Day

Daily Reflection

- What have I done today to commit to my intention?

_____

- Today I am grateful for?

_____

_____

- Today_____brought me joy.

DAILY INTENTION

Date: /   /

Questions to ask yourself today

- What do I need today?
- What is my why?
- What Inspires me?
- What is my heart's deepest desire?
- What do I need to do in order to succeed?
- What obstacles do I need to overcome if any and how will I do this?

Space for thoughts & feelings

Intention of the Day

Daily Reflection

- What have I done today to commit to my intention?

_____

- Today I am grateful for?

_____

_____

- Today_____brought me joy.

DAILY INTENTION

Date: /   /

Questions to ask yourself today

- What do I need today?
- What is my why?
- What Inspires me?
- What is my heart's deepest desire?
- What do I need to do in order to succeed?
- What obstacles do I need to overcome if any and how will I do this?

Space for thoughts & feelings

Intention of the Day

Daily Reflection

- What have I done today to commit to my intention?

_____

- Today I am grateful for?

_____

_____

- Today_____brought me joy.

DAILY INTENTION

Date: /   /

Questions to ask yourself today

- What do I need today?
- What is my why?
- What Inspires me?
- What is my heart's deepest desire?
- What do I need to do in order to succeed?
- What obstacles do I need to overcome if any and how will I do this?

Space for thoughts & feelings

Intention of the Day

Daily Reflection

- What have I done today to commit to my intention?

_____

- Today I am grateful for?

_____

_____

- Today_____brought me joy.

DAILY INTENTION

Date:　　/　　/

Questions to ask yourself today

- What do I need today?
- What is my why?
- What Inspires me?
- What is my heart's deepest desire?
- What do I need to do in order to succeed?
- What obstacles do I need to overcome if any and how will I do this?

Space for thoughts & feelings

Intention of the Day

Daily Reflection

- What have I done today to commit to my intention?

_____

- Today I am grateful for?

_____

_____

- Today_____brought me joy.

DAILY INTENTION

Date: /   /

Questions to ask yourself today

- What do I need today?
- What is my why?
- What Inspires me?
- What is my heart's deepest desire?
- What do I need to do in order to succeed?
- What obstacles do I need to overcome if any and how will I do this?

Space for thoughts & feelings

Intention of the Day

Daily Reflection

- What have I done today to commit to my intention?

_____

- Today I am grateful for?

_____

_____

- Today_____brought me joy.

DAILY INTENTION

Date: / /

Questions to ask yourself today

- What do I need today?
- What is my why?
- What Inspires me?
- What is my heart's deepest desire?
- What do I need to do in order to succeed?
- What obstacles do I need to overcome if any and how will I do this?

Space for thoughts & feelings

Intention of the Day

Daily Reflection

- What have I done today to commit to my intention?

_____

- Today I am grateful for?

_____

_____

- Today_____brought me joy.

DAILY INTENTION

Date: /   /

Questions to ask yourself today

- What do I need today?
- What is my why?
- What Inspires me?
- What is my heart's deepest desire?
- What do I need to do in order to succeed?
- What obstacles do I need to overcome if any and how will I do this?

Space for thoughts & feelings

Intention of the Day

Daily Reflection

- What have I done today to commit to my intention?

_____

- Today I am grateful for?

_____

_____

- Today_____brought me joy.

DAILY INTENTION

Date: /   /

Questions to ask yourself today

- What do I need today?
- What is my why?
- What Inspires me?
- What is my heart's deepest desire?
- What do I need to do in order to succeed?
- What obstacles do I need to overcome if any and how will I do this?

Space for thoughts & feelings

Intention of the Day

Daily Reflection

- What have I done today to commit to my intention?

_____

- Today I am grateful for?

_____

_____

- Today_____brought me joy.

DAILY INTENTION

Date: /   /

Questions to ask yourself today

- What do I need today?
- What is my why?
- What Inspires me?
- What is my heart's deepest desire?
- What do I need to do in order to succeed?
- What obstacles do I need to overcome if any and how will I do this?

Space for thoughts & feelings

Intention of the Day

Daily Reflection

- What have I done today to commit to my intention?

_____

- Today I am grateful for?

_____

_____

- Today_____brought me joy.

DAILY INTENTION

Date: /   /

Questions to ask yourself today

- What do I need today?
- What is my why?
- What Inspires me?
- What is my heart's deepest desire?
- What do I need to do in order to succeed?
- What obstacles do I need to overcome if any and how will I do this?

> *Space for thoughts & feelings*

Intention of the Day

Daily Reflection

- What have I done today to commit to my intention?

_____

- Today I am grateful for?

_____

_____

- Today_____brought me joy.

Date: /   /

Questions to ask yourself today

- What do I need today?
- What is my why?
- What Inspires me?
- What is my heart's deepest desire?
- What do I need to do in order to succeed?
- What obstacles do I need to overcome if any and how will I do this?

Space for thoughts & feelings

Intention of the Day

Daily Reflection

- What have I done today to commit to my intention?

_____

- Today I am grateful for?

_____

_____

- Today_____brought me joy.

DAILY INTENTION

Date: /   /

Questions to ask yourself today

- What do I need today?
- What is my why?
- What Inspires me?
- What is my heart's deepest desire?
- What do I need to do in order to succeed?
- What obstacles do I need to overcome if any and how will I do this?

Space for thoughts & feelings

Intention of the Day

Daily Reflection

- What have I done today to commit to my intention?

_____

- Today I am grateful for?

_____

_____

- Today_____brought me joy.

DAILY INTENTION

Date: /   /

Questions to ask yourself today

- What do I need today?
- What is my why?
- What Inspires me?
- What is my heart's deepest desire?
- What do I need to do in order to succeed?
- What obstacles do I need to overcome if any and how will I do this?

Space for thoughts & feelings

Intention of the Day

Daily Reflection

- What have I done today to commit to my intention?

_____

- Today I am grateful for?

_____

_____

- Today_____brought me joy.

DAILY INTENTION

Date: /   /

Questions to ask yourself today

- What do I need today?
- What is my why?
- What Inspires me?
- What is my heart's deepest desire?
- What do I need to do in order to succeed?
- What obstacles do I need to overcome if any and how will I do this?

Space for thoughts & feelings

Intention of the Day

Daily Reflection

- What have I done today to commit to my intention?

_____

- Today I am grateful for?

_____

_____

- Today_____brought me joy.

DAILY INTENTION

Date: /   /

Questions to ask yourself today

- What do I need today?
- What is my why?
- What Inspires me?
- What is my heart's deepest desire?
- What do I need to do in order to succeed?
- What obstacles do I need to overcome if any and how will I do this?

Space for thoughts & feelings

Intention of the Day

Daily Reflection

- What have I done today to commit to my intention?

_____

- Today I am grateful for?

_____

_____

- Today_____brought me joy.

DAILY INTENTION

Date: /   /

Questions to ask yourself today

- What do I need today?
- What is my why?
- What Inspires me?
- What is my heart's deepest desire?
- What do I need to do in order to succeed?
- What obstacles do I need to overcome if any and how will I do this?

Space for thoughts & feelings

Intention of the Day

Daily Reflection

- What have I done today to commit to my intention?

_____

- Today I am grateful for?

_____

_____

- Today_____brought me joy.

DAILY INTENTION

Date: /   /

Questions to ask yourself today

- What do I need today?
- What is my why?
- What Inspires me?
- What is my heart's deepest desire?
- What do I need to do in order to succeed?
- What obstacles do I need to overcome if any and how will I do this?

Space for thoughts & feelings

Intention of the Day

Daily Reflection

- What have I done today to commit to my intention?

_____

- Today I am grateful for?

_____

_____

- Today_____brought me joy.

DAILY INTENTION

Date: /   /

Questions to ask yourself today

- What do I need today?
- What is my why?
- What Inspires me?
- What is my heart's deepest desire?
- What do I need to do in order to succeed?
- What obstacles do I need to overcome if any and how will I do this?

Space for thoughts & feelings

Intention of the Day

Daily Reflection

- What have I done today to commit to my intention?

_____

- Today I am grateful for?

_____

_____

- Today_____brought me joy.

DAILY INTENTION

Date: /   /

Questions to ask yourself today

- What do I need today?
- What is my why?
- What Inspires me?
- What is my heart's deepest desire?
- What do I need to do in order to succeed?
- What obstacles do I need to overcome if any and how will I do this?

Space for thoughts & feelings

Intention of the Day

Daily Reflection

- What have I done today to commit to my intention?

_____

- Today I am grateful for?

_____

_____

- Today_____brought me joy.

DAILY INTENTION

Date: /   /

Questions to ask yourself today

- What do I need today?
- What is my why?
- What Inspires me?
- What is my heart's deepest desire?
- What do I need to do in order to succeed?
- What obstacles do I need to overcome if any and how will I do this?

Space for thoughts & feelings

Intention of the Day

Daily Reflection

- What have I done today to commit to my intention?

_____

- Today I am grateful for?

_____

_____

- Today_____brought me joy.

Date: /   /

Questions to ask yourself today

- What do I need today?
- What is my why?
- What Inspires me?
- What is my heart's deepest desire?
- What do I need to do in order to succeed?
- What obstacles do I need to overcome if any and how will I do this?

Space for thoughts & feelings

Intention of the Day

Daily Reflection

- What have I done today to commit to my intention?

_____

- Today I am grateful for?

_____

_____

- Today_____brought me joy.

DAILY INTENTION

Date: /   /

Questions to ask yourself today

- What do I need today?
- What is my why?
- What Inspires me?
- What is my heart's deepest desire?
- What do I need to do in order to succeed?
- What obstacles do I need to overcome if any and how will I do this?

Space for thoughts & feelings

Intention of the Day

Daily Reflection

- What have I done today to commit to my intention?

_____

- Today I am grateful for?

_____

_____

- Today_____brought me joy.

DAILY INTENTION

Date: /   /

Questions to ask yourself today

- What do I need today?
- What is my why?
- What Inspires me?
- What is my heart's deepest desire?
- What do I need to do in order to succeed?
- What obstacles do I need to overcome if any and how will I do this?

Space for thoughts & feelings

Intention of the Day

Daily Reflection

- What have I done today to commit to my intention?

_____

- Today I am grateful for?

_____

_____

- Today_____brought me joy.

DAILY INTENTION

Date: /   /

Questions to ask yourself today

- What do I need today?
- What is my why?
- What Inspires me?
- What is my heart's deepest desire?
- What do I need to do in order to succeed?
- What obstacles do I need to overcome if any and how will I do this?

Space for thoughts & feelings

Intention of the Day

Daily Reflection

- What have I done today to commit to my intention?

_____

- Today I am grateful for?

_____

_____

- Today_____brought me joy.

DAILY INTENTION

Date: /   /

Questions to ask yourself today

- What do I need today?
- What is my why?
- What Inspires me?
- What is my heart's deepest desire?
- What do I need to do in order to succeed?
- What obstacles do I need to overcome if any and how will I do this?

> *Space for thoughts & feelings*

Intention of the Day

Daily Reflection

- What have I done today to commit to my intention?

_____

- Today I am grateful for?

_____

_____

- Today_____brought me joy.

DAILY INTENTION

Date: /   /

Questions to ask yourself today

- What do I need today?
- What is my why?
- What Inspires me?
- What is my heart's deepest desire?
- What do I need to do in order to succeed?
- What obstacles do I need to overcome if any and how will I do this?

Space for thoughts & feelings

Intention of the Day

Daily Reflection

- What have I done today to commit to my intention?

_____

- Today I am grateful for?

_____

_____

- Today_____brought me joy.

DAILY INTENTION

Date: /   /

Questions to ask yourself today

- What do I need today?
- What is my why?
- What Inspires me?
- What is my heart's deepest desire?
- What do I need to do in order to succeed?
- What obstacles do I need to overcome if any and how will I do this?

Space for thoughts & feelings

Intention of the Day

Daily Reflection

- What have I done today to commit to my intention?

_____

- Today I am grateful for?

_____

_____

- Today_____brought me joy.

DAILY INTENTION

Date: /   /

Questions to ask yourself today

- What do I need today?
- What is my why?
- What Inspires me?
- What is my heart's deepest desire?
- What do I need to do in order to succeed?
- What obstacles do I need to overcome if any and how will I do this?

> *Space for thoughts & feelings*

> **Intention of the Day**

Daily Reflection

- What have I done today to commit to my intention?

_____

- Today I am grateful for?

_____

_____

- Today_____brought me joy.

DAILY INTENTION

Date: /   /

Questions to ask yourself today

- What do I need today?
- What is my why?
- What Inspires me?
- What is my heart's deepest desire?
- What do I need to do in order to succeed?
- What obstacles do I need to overcome if any and how will I do this?

> Space for thoughts & feelings

Intention of the Day

Daily Reflection

- What have I done today to commit to my intention?

_____

- Today I am grateful for?

_____

_____

- Today_____brought me joy.

DAILY INTENTION

Date: /   /

Questions to ask yourself today

- What do I need today?
- What is my why?
- What Inspires me?
- What is my heart's deepest desire?
- What do I need to do in order to succeed?
- What obstacles do I need to overcome if any and how will I do this?

Space for thoughts & feelings

Intention of the Day

Daily Reflection

- What have I done today to commit to my intention?

_____

- Today I am grateful for?

_____

_____

- Today_____brought me joy.

DAILY INTENTION

Date: /   /

Questions to ask yourself today

- What do I need today?
- What is my why?
- What Inspires me?
- What is my heart's deepest desire?
- What do I need to do in order to succeed?
- What obstacles do I need to overcome if any and how will I do this?

Space for thoughts & feelings

Intention of the Day

Daily Reflection

- What have I done today to commit to my intention?

_____

- Today I am grateful for?

_____

_____

- Today_____brought me joy.

DAILY INTENTION

Date: /   /

Questions to ask yourself today

- What do I need today?
- What is my why?
- What Inspires me?
- What is my heart's deepest desire?
- What do I need to do in order to succeed?
- What obstacles do I need to overcome if any and how will I do this?

> *Space for thoughts & feelings*

Intention of the Day

Daily Reflection

- What have I done today to commit to my intention?

_____

- Today I am grateful for?

_____

_____

- Today_____brought me joy.

DAILY INTENTION

Date: /   /

Questions to ask yourself today

- What do I need today?
- What is my why?
- What Inspires me?
- What is my heart's deepest desire?
- What do I need to do in order to succeed?
- What obstacles do I need to overcome if any and how will I do this?

> *Space for thoughts & feelings*

> **Intention of the Day**

Daily Reflection

- What have I done today to commit to my intention?

_____

- Today I am grateful for?

_____

_____

- Today_____brought me joy.

DAILY INTENTION

Date: /   /

Questions to ask yourself today

- What do I need today?
- What is my why?
- What Inspires me?
- What is my heart's deepest desire?
- What do I need to do in order to succeed?
- What obstacles do I need to overcome if any and how will I do this?

> *Space for thoughts & feelings*

Intention of the Day

Daily Reflection

- What have I done today to commit to my intention?

_____

- Today I am grateful for?

_____

_____

- Today_____brought me joy.

DAILY INTENTION

Date: /   /

Questions to ask yourself today

- What do I need today?
- What is my why?
- What Inspires me?
- What is my heart's deepest desire?
- What do I need to do in order to succeed?
- What obstacles do I need to overcome if any and how will I do this?

Space for thoughts & feelings

Intention of the Day

Daily Reflection

- What have I done today to commit to my intention?

_____

- Today I am grateful for?

_____

_____

- Today_____brought me joy.

DAILY INTENTION

Date:　　　/　　　/

Questions to ask yourself today

- What do I need today?
- What is my why?
- What Inspires me?
- What is my heart's deepest desire?
- What do I need to do in order to succeed?
- What obstacles do I need to overcome if any and how will I do this?

Space for thoughts & feelings

Intention of the Day

Daily Reflection

- What have I done today to commit to my intention?

_____

- Today I am grateful for?

_____

_____

- Today_____brought me joy.

DAILY INTENTION

Date: /   /

Questions to ask yourself today

- What do I need today?
- What is my why?
- What Inspires me?
- What is my heart's deepest desire?
- What do I need to do in order to succeed?
- What obstacles do I need to overcome if any and how will I do this?

> *Space for thoughts & feelings*

Intention of the Day

Daily Reflection

- What have I done today to commit to my intention?

_____

- Today I am grateful for?

_____

_____

- Today_____brought me joy.

DAILY INTENTION

Date: /   /

Questions to ask yourself today

- What do I need today?
- What is my why?
- What Inspires me?
- What is my heart's deepest desire?
- What do I need to do in order to succeed?
- What obstacles do I need to overcome if any and how will I do this?

> *Space for thoughts & feelings*

Intention of the Day

Daily Reflection

- What have I done today to commit to my intention?

_____

- Today I am grateful for?

_____

_____

- Today_____brought me joy.

DAILY INTENTION

Date: /   /

Questions to ask yourself today

- What do I need today?
- What is my why?
- What Inspires me?
- What is my heart's deepest desire?
- What do I need to do in order to succeed?
- What obstacles do I need to overcome if any and how will I do this?

Space for thoughts & feelings

Intention of the Day

Daily Reflection

- What have I done today to commit to my intention?

_____

- Today I am grateful for?

_____

_____

- Today_____brought me joy.

DAILY INTENTION

Date: /   /

Questions to ask yourself today

- What do I need today?
- What is my why?
- What Inspires me?
- What is my heart's deepest desire?
- What do I need to do in order to succeed?
- What obstacles do I need to overcome if any and how will I do this?

> *Space for thoughts & feelings*

Intention of the Day

Daily Reflection

- What have I done today to commit to my intention?

_____

- Today I am grateful for?

_____

_____

- Today_____brought me joy.

DAILY INTENTION

Date: /   /

Questions to ask yourself today

- What do I need today?
- What is my why?
- What Inspires me?
- What is my heart's deepest desire?
- What do I need to do in order to succeed?
- What obstacles do I need to overcome if any and how will I do this?

Space for thoughts & feelings

Intention of the Day

Daily Reflection

- What have I done today to commit to my intention?

_____

- Today I am grateful for?

_____

_____

- Today_____brought me joy.

DAILY INTENTION

Date: /   /

Questions to ask yourself today

- What do I need today?
- What is my why?
- What Inspires me?
- What is my heart's deepest desire?
- What do I need to do in order to succeed?
- What obstacles do I need to overcome if any and how will I do this?

Space for thoughts & feelings

Intention of the Day

Daily Reflection

- What have I done today to commit to my intention?

_____

- Today I am grateful for?

_____

_____

- Today_____brought me joy.

DAILY INTENTION

Date: /   /

Questions to ask yourself today

- What do I need today?
- What is my why?
- What Inspires me?
- What is my heart's deepest desire?
- What do I need to do in order to succeed?
- What obstacles do I need to overcome if any and how will I do this?

> *Space for thoughts & feelings*

Intention of the Day

Daily Reflection

- What have I done today to commit to my intention?

_____

- Today I am grateful for?

_____

_____

- Today_____brought me joy.

DAILY INTENTION

Date: /   /

Questions to ask yourself today

- What do I need today?
- What is my why?
- What Inspires me?
- What is my heart's deepest desire?
- What do I need to do in order to succeed?
- What obstacles do I need to overcome if any and how will I do this?

Space for thoughts & feelings

Intention of the Day

Daily Reflection

- What have I done today to commit to my intention?

_____

- Today I am grateful for?

_____

_____

- Today_____brought me joy.

Date: /   /

Questions to ask yourself today

- What do I need today?
- What is my why?
- What Inspires me?
- What is my heart's deepest desire?
- What do I need to do in order to succeed?
- What obstacles do I need to overcome if any and how will I do this?

Space for thoughts & feelings

Intention of the Day

Daily Reflection

- What have I done today to commit to my intention?

_____

- Today I am grateful for?

_____

_____

- Today_____brought me joy.

DAILY INTENTION

Date: /   /

Questions to ask yourself today

- What do I need today?
- What is my why?
- What Inspires me?
- What is my heart's deepest desire?
- What do I need to do in order to succeed?
- What obstacles do I need to overcome if any and how will I do this?

Space for thoughts & feelings

Intention of the Day

Daily Reflection

- What have I done today to commit to my intention?

_____

- Today I am grateful for?

_____

_____

- Today_____brought me joy.

DAILY INTENTION

Date: /   /

Questions to ask yourself today

- What do I need today?
- What is my why?
- What Inspires me?
- What is my heart's deepest desire?
- What do I need to do in order to succeed?
- What obstacles do I need to overcome if any and how will I do this?

Space for thoughts & feelings

Intention of the Day

Daily Reflection

- What have I done today to commit to my intention?

_____

- Today I am grateful for?

_____

_____

- Today_____brought me joy.

DAILY INTENTION

Date: /   /

Questions to ask yourself today

- What do I need today?
- What is my why?
- What Inspires me?
- What is my heart's deepest desire?
- What do I need to do in order to succeed?
- What obstacles do I need to overcome if any and how will I do this?

Space for thoughts & feelings

Intention of the Day

Daily Reflection

- What have I done today to commit to my intention?

_____

- Today I am grateful for?

_____

_____

- Today_____brought me joy.

DAILY INTENTION

Date: /   /

Questions to ask yourself today

- What do I need today?
- What is my why?
- What Inspires me?
- What is my heart's deepest desire?
- What do I need to do in order to succeed?
- What obstacles do I need to overcome if any and how will I do this?

Space for thoughts & feelings

Intention of the Day

Daily Reflection

- What have I done today to commit to my intention?

_____

- Today I am grateful for?

_____

_____

- Today_____brought me joy.

DAILY INTENTION

Date: /   /

Questions to ask yourself today

- What do I need today?
- What is my why?
- What Inspires me?
- What is my heart's deepest desire?
- What do I need to do in order to succeed?
- What obstacles do I need to overcome if any and how will I do this?

Space for thoughts & feelings

Intention of the Day

Daily Reflection

- What have I done today to commit to my intention?

_____

- Today I am grateful for?

_____

_____

- Today_____brought me joy.

DAILY INTENTION

Date: /   /

Questions to ask yourself today

- What do I need today?
- What is my why?
- What Inspires me?
- What is my heart's deepest desire?
- What do I need to do in order to succeed?
- What obstacles do I need to overcome if any and how will I do this?

Space for thoughts & feelings

Intention of the Day

Daily Reflection

- What have I done today to commit to my intention?

_____

- Today I am grateful for?

_____

_____

- Today_____brought me joy.

DAILY INTENTION

Date: /   /

Questions to ask yourself today

- What do I need today?
- What is my why?
- What Inspires me?
- What is my heart's deepest desire?
- What do I need to do in order to succeed?
- What obstacles do I need to overcome if any and how will I do this?

Space for thoughts & feelings

Intention of the Day

Daily Reflection

- What have I done today to commit to my intention?

_____

- Today I am grateful for?

_____

_____

- Today_____brought me joy.

DAILY INTENTION

Date: /   /

Questions to ask yourself today

- What do I need today?
- What is my why?
- What Inspires me?
- What is my heart's deepest desire?
- What do I need to do in order to succeed?
- What obstacles do I need to overcome if any and how will I do this?

Space for thoughts & feelings

Intention of the Day

Daily Reflection

- What have I done today to commit to my intention?

_____

- Today I am grateful for?

_____

_____

- Today_____brought me joy.

DAILY INTENTION

Date: /   /

Questions to ask yourself today

- What do I need today?
- What is my why?
- What Inspires me?
- What is my heart's deepest desire?
- What do I need to do in order to succeed?
- What obstacles do I need to overcome if any and how will I do this?

Space for thoughts & feelings

Intention of the Day

Daily Reflection

- What have I done today to commit to my intention?

_____

- Today I am grateful for?

_____

_____

- Today_____brought me joy.

DAILY INTENTION

Date: /   /

Questions to ask yourself today

- What do I need today?
- What is my why?
- What Inspires me?
- What is my heart's deepest desire?
- What do I need to do in order to succeed?
- What obstacles do I need to overcome if any and how will I do this?

Space for thoughts & feelings

Intention of the Day

Daily Reflection

- What have I done today to commit to my intention?

_____

- Today I am grateful for?

_____

_____

- Today_____brought me joy.

DAILY INTENTION

Date: /   /

Questions to ask yourself today

- What do I need today?
- What is my why?
- What Inspires me?
- What is my heart's deepest desire?
- What do I need to do in order to succeed?
- What obstacles do I need to overcome if any and how will I do this?

Space for thoughts & feelings

Intention of the Day

Daily Reflection

- What have I done today to commit to my intention?

_____

- Today I am grateful for?

_____

_____

- Today_____brought me joy.

DAILY INTENTION

Date: /   /

Questions to ask yourself today

- What do I need today?
- What is my why?
- What Inspires me?
- What is my heart's deepest desire?
- What do I need to do in order to succeed?
- What obstacles do I need to overcome if any and how will I do this?

Space for thoughts & feelings

Intention of the Day

Daily Reflection

- What have I done today to commit to my intention?

_____

- Today I am grateful for?

_____

_____

- Today_____brought me joy.

DAILY INTENTION

Date: /   /

Questions to ask yourself today

- What do I need today?
- What is my why?
- What Inspires me?
- What is my heart's deepest desire?
- What do I need to do in order to succeed?
- What obstacles do I need to overcome if any and how will I do this?

> *Space for thoughts & feelings*

Intention of the Day

Daily Reflection

- What have I done today to commit to my intention?

_____

- Today I am grateful for?

_____

_____

- Today_____brought me joy.

DAILY INTENTION

Date: /   /

Questions to ask yourself today

- What do I need today?
- What is my why?
- What Inspires me?
- What is my heart's deepest desire?
- What do I need to do in order to succeed?
- What obstacles do I need to overcome if any and how will I do this?

> *Space for thoughts & feelings*

Intention of the Day

Daily Reflection

- What have I done today to commit to my intention?

_____

- Today I am grateful for?

_____

_____

- Today_____brought me joy.

DAILY INTENTION

Date: /   /

Questions to ask yourself today

- What do I need today?
- What is my why?
- What Inspires me?
- What is my heart's deepest desire?
- What do I need to do in order to succeed?
- What obstacles do I need to overcome if any and how will I do this?

Space for thoughts & feelings

Intention of the Day

Daily Reflection

- What have I done today to commit to my intention?

_____

- Today I am grateful for?

_____

_____

- Today_____brought me joy.

DAILY INTENTION

Date: /   /

Questions to ask yourself today

- What do I need today?
- What is my why?
- What Inspires me?
- What is my heart's deepest desire?
- What do I need to do in order to succeed?
- What obstacles do I need to overcome if any and how will I do this?

> *Space for thoughts & feelings*

Intention of the Day

Daily Reflection

- What have I done today to commit to my intention?

_____

- Today I am grateful for?

_____

_____

- Today_____brought me joy.

DAILY INTENTION

Date: /   /

Questions to ask yourself today

- What do I need today?
- What is my why?
- What Inspires me?
- What is my heart's deepest desire?
- What do I need to do in order to succeed?
- What obstacles do I need to overcome if any and how will I do this?

Space for thoughts & feelings

Intention of the Day

Daily Reflection

- What have I done today to commit to my intention?

_____

- Today I am grateful for?

_____

_____

- Today_____brought me joy.

DAILY INTENTION

Date: /   /

Questions to ask yourself today

- What do I need today?
- What is my why?
- What Inspires me?
- What is my heart's deepest desire?
- What do I need to do in order to succeed?
- What obstacles do I need to overcome if any and how will I do this?

> Space for thoughts & feelings

Intention of the Day

Daily Reflection

- What have I done today to commit to my intention?

_____

- Today I am grateful for?

_____

_____

- Today_____brought me joy.

DAILY INTENTION

Date: /   /

Questions to ask yourself today

- What do I need today?
- What is my why?
- What Inspires me?
- What is my heart's deepest desire?
- What do I need to do in order to succeed?
- What obstacles do I need to overcome if any and how will I do this?

Space for thoughts & feelings

Intention of the Day

Daily Reflection

- What have I done today to commit to my intention?

_____

- Today I am grateful for?

_____

_____

- Today_____brought me joy.

DAILY INTENTION

Date: /   /

Questions to ask yourself today

- What do I need today?
- What is my why?
- What Inspires me?
- What is my heart's deepest desire?
- What do I need to do in order to succeed?
- What obstacles do I need to overcome if any and how will I do this?

Space for thoughts & feelings

Intention of the Day

Daily Reflection

- What have I done today to commit to my intention?

_____

- Today I am grateful for?

_____

_____

- Today_____brought me joy.

DAILY INTENTION

Date: /   /

Questions to ask yourself today

- What do I need today?
- What is my why?
- What Inspires me?
- What is my heart's deepest desire?
- What do I need to do in order to succeed?
- What obstacles do I need to overcome if any and how will I do this?

Space for thoughts & feelings

Intention of the Day

Daily Reflection

- What have I done today to commit to my intention?

_____

- Today I am grateful for?

_____

_____

- Today_____brought me joy.

DAILY INTENTION

Date: / /

Questions to ask yourself today

- What do I need today?
- What is my why?
- What Inspires me?
- What is my heart's deepest desire?
- What do I need to do in order to succeed?
- What obstacles do I need to overcome if any and how will I do this?

Space for thoughts & feelings

Intention of the Day

Daily Reflection

- What have I done today to commit to my intention?

_____

- Today I am grateful for?

_____

_____

- Today_____brought me joy.

DAILY INTENTION

Date: /   /

Questions to ask yourself today

- What do I need today?
- What is my why?
- What Inspires me?
- What is my heart's deepest desire?
- What do I need to do in order to succeed?
- What obstacles do I need to overcome if any and how will I do this?

Space for thoughts & feelings

Intention of the Day

Daily Reflection

- What have I done today to commit to my intention?

_____

- Today I am grateful for?

_____

_____

- Today_____brought me joy.

Date: /   /

Questions to ask yourself today

- What do I need today?
- What is my why?
- What Inspires me?
- What is my heart's deepest desire?
- What do I need to do in order to succeed?
- What obstacles do I need to overcome if any and how will I do this?

Space for thoughts & feelings

Intention of the Day

Daily Reflection

- What have I done today to commit to my intention?

_____

- Today I am grateful for?

_____

_____

- Today_____brought me joy.

WEEKLY

REFLECTIONS

Week ending: /   /

Look back through your previous week's Intentions:
- What have you learnt from these intentions?
- What feelings, ideas and/or realisations have come from your intentions?
- How do you take these learnings forward with you?

Space for thoughts & feelings

Week ending: /   /

Look back through your previous week's Intentions:
- What have you learnt from these intentions?
- What feelings, ideas and/or realisations have come from your intentions?
- How do you take these learnings forward with you?

Space for thoughts & feelings

WEEKLY REFLECTION

Week ending: /   /

Look back through your previous week's Intentions:
- What have you learnt from these intentions?
- What feelings, ideas and/or realisations have come from your intentions?
- How do you take these learnings forward with you?

Space for thoughts & feelings

Week ending: /   /

Look back through your previous week's Intentions:
- What have you learnt from these intentions?
- What feelings, ideas and/or realisations have come from your intentions?
- How do you take these learnings forward with you?

Space for thoughts & feelings

WEEKLY REFLECTION

Week ending: /   /

Look back through your previous week's Intentions:
- What have you learnt from these intentions?
- What feelings, ideas and/or realisations have come from your intentions?
- How do you take these learnings forward with you?

Space for thoughts & feelings

Week ending: /   /

Look back through your previous week's Intentions:
- What have you learnt from these intentions?
- What feelings, ideas and/or realisations have come from your intentions?
- How do you take these learnings forward with you?

Space for thoughts & feelings

WEEKLY REFLECTION

Week ending: /   /

Look back through your previous week's Intentions:
- What have you learnt from these intentions?
- What feelings, ideas and/or realisations have come from your intentions?
- How do you take these learnings forward with you?

> *Space for thoughts & feelings*

Week ending: /   /

Look back through your previous week's Intentions:
- What have you learnt from these intentions?
- What feelings, ideas and/or realisations have come from your intentions?
- How do you take these learnings forward with you?

> *Space for thoughts & feelings*

Week ending: /   /

Look back through your previous week's Intentions:
- What have you learnt from these intentions?
- What feelings, ideas and/or realisations have come from your intentions?
- How do you take these learnings forward with you?

Space for thoughts & feelings

Week ending: /   /

Look back through your previous week's Intentions:
- What have you learnt from these intentions?
- What feelings, ideas and/or realisations have come from your intentions?
- How do you take these learnings forward with you?

Space for thoughts & feelings

Week ending: /   /

Look back through your previous week's Intentions:
- What have you learnt from these intentions?
- What feelings, ideas and/or realisations have come from your intentions?
- How do you take these learnings forward with you?

Space for thoughts & feelings

Week ending: /   /

Look back through your previous week's Intentions:
- What have you learnt from these intentions?
- What feelings, ideas and/or realisations have come from your intentions?
- How do you take these learnings forward with you?

Space for thoughts & feelings

Week ending: /   /

Look back through your previous week's Intentions:
- What have you learnt from these intentions?
- What feelings, ideas and/or realisations have come from your intentions?
- How do you take these learnings forward with you?

Space for thoughts & feelings

Week ending: /   /

Look back through your previous week's Intentions:
- What have you learnt from these intentions?
- What feelings, ideas and/or realisations have come from your intentions?
- How do you take these learnings forward with you?

Space for thoughts & feelings

Week ending: /   /

Look back through your previous week's Intentions:
- What have you learnt from these intentions?
- What feelings, ideas and/or realisations have come from your intentions?
- How do you take these learnings forward with you?

Space for thoughts & feelings

Week ending: /   /

Look back through your previous week's Intentions:
- What have you learnt from these intentions?
- What feelings, ideas and/or realisations have come from your intentions?
- How do you take these learnings forward with you?

Space for thoughts & feelings

Week ending: /   /

Look back through your previous week's Intentions:
- What have you learnt from these intentions?
- What feelings, ideas and/or realisations have come from your intentions?
- How do you take these learnings forward with you?

Space for thoughts & feelings

Week ending: /   /

Look back through your previous week's Intentions:
- What have you learnt from these intentions?
- What feelings, ideas and/or realisations have come from your intentions?
- How do you take these learnings forward with you?

Space for thoughts & feelings

WEEKLY REFLECTION

Week ending: /   /

Look back through your previous week's Intentions:
- What have you learnt from these intentions?
- What feelings, ideas and/or realisations have come from your intentions?
- How do you take these learnings forward with you?

Space for thoughts & feelings

Week ending: /   /

Look back through your previous week's Intentions:
- What have you learnt from these intentions?
- What feelings, ideas and/or realisations have come from your intentions?
- How do you take these learnings forward with you?

Space for thoughts & feelings

Week ending: /   /

Look back through your previous week's Intentions:
- What have you learnt from these intentions?
- What feelings, ideas and/or realisations have come from your intentions?
- How do you take these learnings forward with you?

Space for thoughts & feelings

Week ending: /   /

Look back through your previous week's Intentions:
- What have you learnt from these intentions?
- What feelings, ideas and/or realisations have come from your intentions?
- How do you take these learnings forward with you?

Space for thoughts & feelings

Week ending: /   /

Look back through your previous week's Intentions:
- What have you learnt from these intentions?
- What feelings, ideas and/or realisations have come from your intentions?
- How do you take these learnings forward with you?

> *Space for thoughts & feelings*

Week ending: /   /

Look back through your previous week's Intentions:
- What have you learnt from these intentions?
- What feelings, ideas and/or realisations have come from your intentions?
- How do you take these learnings forward with you?

> *Space for thoughts & feelings*

WEEKLY REFLECTION

Week ending: /   /

Look back through your previous week's Intentions:

- What have you learnt from these intentions?
- What feelings, ideas and/or realisations have come from your intentions?
- How do you take these learnings forward with you?

> *Space for thoughts & feelings*

Week ending: /   /

Look back through your previous week's Intentions:

- What have you learnt from these intentions?
- What feelings, ideas and/or realisations have come from your intentions?
- How do you take these learnings forward with you?

> *Space for thoughts & feelings*

WEEKLY REFLECTION

Week ending: /   /

Look back through your previous week's Intentions:
- What have you learnt from these intentions?
- What feelings, ideas and/or realisations have come from your intentions?
- How do you take these learnings forward with you?

> *Space for thoughts & feelings*

Week ending: /   /

Look back through your previous week's Intentions:
- What have you learnt from these intentions?
- What feelings, ideas and/or realisations have come from your intentions?
- How do you take these learnings forward with you?

> *Space for thoughts & feelings*

WEEKLY REFLECTION

Week ending: /   /

Look back through your previous week's Intentions:
- What have you learnt from these intentions?
- What feelings, ideas and/or realisations have come from your intentions?
- How do you take these learnings forward with you?

Space for thoughts & feelings

Week ending: /   /

Look back through your previous week's Intentions:
- What have you learnt from these intentions?
- What feelings, ideas and/or realisations have come from your intentions?
- How do you take these learnings forward with you?

Space for thoughts & feelings

WEEKLY REFLECTION

Week ending: /   /

Look back through your previous week's Intentions:

- What have you learnt from these intentions?
- What feelings, ideas and/or realisations have come from your intentions?
- How do you take these learnings forward with you?

> *Space for thoughts & feelings*

Week ending: /   /

Look back through your previous week's Intentions:

- What have you learnt from these intentions?
- What feelings, ideas and/or realisations have come from your intentions?
- How do you take these learnings forward with you?

> *Space for thoughts & feelings*

Printed in Great Britain
by Amazon